GOD'S RAINBOW HAS SEVEN COLORS LET ME TELL YOU WHAT IT MEANS

1

RED

The first color of the rainbow is red. It stands for LOVE.

Love is patient, love is kind. It does not envy, it does not boast, it is not proud.

1 Corinthians 13:4

2

ORANGE

THE SECOND COLOR OF THE RAINBOW IS ORANGE

IT STANDS FOR JOY

The joy of the LORD is your strength."
Nehemiah 8:10

3

YELLOW

**THE THIRD COLOR
OF THE RAINBOW
IS YELLOW'
IT STANDS FOR
LIGHT**

The Light shines in the darkness. The darkness has never been able to put out the Light.

John 1:4

4

GREEN

THE FOURTH COLOR OF THE RAINBOW IS GREEN. IT STANDS FOR NATURE.

And God said, Let the earth bring forth grass, the herb yielding seed, and the fruit tree yielding fruit after his kind, whose seed is in itself, upon the earth: and it was so.

Genesis 1:11

5

BLUE

THE FIFTH COLOR OF THE RAINBOW IS BLUE. IT STANDS FOR STABILITY

Therefore, my beloved brethren, be stedfast, unmoveable, always abounding in the work of the Lord, forasmuch as you know that your labour is not in vain in the Lord.

1 Corinthians 15:58

6

INDIGO

**THE SIXTH COLOR OF THE RAINBOW IS INDIGO.
IT STANDS
FOR SPIRITUALITY**

**For to be carnally minded is death;
but to be
spiritually minded is life and peace.
Romans 8:6**

7

VIOLET

THE SEVENTH COLOR OF THE RAINBOW IS VIOLET IT STANDS FOR ROYALTY

But you are a chosen people, a royal priesthood, a holy nation, God's special possession, that you may declare the praises of him who called you out of darkness into his wonderful light.

1 Peter 2:9

The rainbow we see in the sky
belongs to God. It has many
colors but only seven are
visible to the eyes.

NOW WHEN YOU SEE GOD'S RAINBOW UP IN THE SKY, YOU KNOW EXACTLY WHAT THE BEAUTIFUL COLORS STAND FOR.

"I have set my rainbow in the clouds, and it will be the sign of the covenant between me and the earth."
Genesis 9:13

www.ingramcontent.com/pod-product-compliance
Lightning Source LLC
Chambersburg PA
CBHW041706160426
43209CB00017B/1763
9781734963199